# The Power Pop Investor
*Small Investors Technical Approach to Trading Stock*
By Don L. Markham © 2013

**About the Author.** In the late nineteen eighties, by law I had to use a Full Service Brokerage Service. I won't mention their name but I can tell you the "account managers" did well financially. The most I ever paid for a trade back then was one hundred and eighty seven dollars, that's right $187.00. The least was around forty seven dollars. To make any money you had to buy in large lots of at least one hundred shares. And even small amounts of shares did not lower the cost enough to warrant making any trading mistakes. Everything has changed because of the Internet. The longer we have the internet the more trading will be accessible to everyone. So now days, all you need is to develop your trading method and stick to it.

Table of Contents:

Introduction: *There is no easy answer.*
Chapter One: *Indicators and their use in every day trading.*
Chapter Two: *Actual chart information and explanation.*
Chapter Three: *The Chart's main graphic section.*
Chapter Four: *The lower Indicator section.*
Chapter Five: *The Chart Attributes section.*
Chapter Six: *The Dow Theory*
Chapter Seven: *Thoughts and Ramblings*
Chapter Eight: *Follow Up Information*
Chapter Nine: *The Kiss and Tell Phenomenon*
Chapter 10: *How Hard Do You Want to Work?*

## INTRODUCTION

All Traders Real & Potential: This book is primarily set up for small investors with portfolio investing capabilities from three hundred to five thousand dollars. I am using three thousand dollars as the portfolio size in this book. If you only have five hundred to begin your portfolio then make your trades one sixth the amount of mine. If you have more than five thousand, just up the share amount percentages to equal your monitory size. For instance, if you are investing twelve thousand than just quadruple the size of my trades.

I am taking the opportunity right here to instruct the individuals who think or have been told that this or any other stock trading method is a "get rich quick proposition", that they have been misled. This business, like any other in which I have participated, takes due diligence and a lot of expended effort. It involves hard work and an investment of time and money. If you are not willing to study and work then this book will have less value for you. I also want to mention a fact that should be obvious to all traders; here is where you get the obligatory statement regarding that fact. Your personality and mine may be different enough that my methods will not work for you. I am of the impression that if you do what I do with the correct timing and the proper trade entry and exit points, then you will succeed. With that statement duly entered, we can direct our attention to the process.

I use Scottrade ® as my trading platform in this book. Remember, at Scottrade ® you will be charged seven dollars per trade, so figure that amount into your purchase price, and add it to your selling price. With small portfolios your money will grow by the same percentages but it will take you a lot longer to build your wealth. No, you won't make much money, but the percentages are the same and you will eventually have a sizeable portfolio. Thirty percent of a million dollar trade is the same increase as thirty percent of a one hundred dollar trade. The latter is just not near as much cash in the pocket.

The information in this book is for educational purposes only and should not be construed as a recommendation to buy or sell the stocks mentioned, because trading amounts must be studied daily and acted on when the time arrives. If you use my web site and do your home work then you may be able to duplicate my successes. Hopefully successes will be much larger than failures.

**My Trading Philosophy**. I remember from other market corrections both great and small, that some stocks did well in those markets. No longer am I going to worry about a big market correction where the market drops precipitously. I will keep my trades in line with my research. If a stock is a sell or a buy it will be confirmed by the technical and fundamental research. No more trying to predict the market. I will adhere to the Dow Theory in order to know whether the market is strong or week. I am going to explain my processes step by step and keep the instructions as simple as possible. You can study the trading methods then keep current by visiting my web site daily. I will show a running total of my trades there. I will also have the Dow Theory available for your edification.

**The Beginning:** The Dow Theory and its market tracking powers. The theory quoted from Wikipedia, "The Dow theory on stock price movement is a form of technical analysis that includes some aspects of sector rotation. The theory was derived from 255 Wall Street Journal editorials written by Charles H. Dow (1851–1902), journalist, founder and first editor of the Wall Street Journal and co-founder of Dow Jones and Company. Following Dow's death, William Peter Hamilton, Robert Rhea and E. George Schaefer organized and collectively represented Dow Theory, based on Dow's editorials. Dow himself never used the term Dow Theory nor presented it as a trading system..." "Wikipedia."

Another factor that excites me is the inter relatedness of the two components of the theory. The DJIA and TRAN (transportation). John Murphy the master mind behind Stockcharts.com ® theorized and then through, extensive research, proved his theory to the satisfaction of most traders. That not just world stock markets but all markets are interrelated. So, as Charles Dow wrote, transportation drives the Dow. Other things help but transportation is the big dog chasing that seems to help the DJIA trend.

Following is an example of the pre-Christmas trade 12/15/2013: 12/21/2013 it has been an unbelievable market for the past few months. By watching The Dow Theory you could tell that our money people knew that things were not dire just grievous. Friday, 13 was some relief from the down trend.  Now we have to worry about lower lows and lower highs.  Higher highs and higher lows are very good because they forecast a bull trend.  I can't predict but I can certainly follow my research.  It is not looking good but it beats the alternative of being all bad.  Commodity Channel Index (CCI) came back a little but is still negative. Relative Strength Index (RSI) is also negative. Daily Moving Averages (DMAs) are positive but above the price line which is not good.  Average Directional Index (ADX), TRIX, Moving Average Convergence/Divergence (MACD) and Stochastic are giving negative information. But, look at $Trans Transportation), Just Trucking and hauling right on up.  12/21: more of the good stuff.  Looking for a new higher high.

**The Starting Place.**  There are many entities that are very good at finding the viable tradable companies.  Currently, my favorite is "WSD Insider".  I subscribe to this service because, in my opinion, they are as good as or better than any out there.  If you decide to follow my site then you will not need to subscribe because I am using their information as part of my research.  It is not expensive for an annual subscription so you may want to purchase a membership anyway.

You may also wish to subscribe to StockCharts.com.  This site is simply the best charting program available.  It is a free site but if you become a serious investor you will want to buy a subscription.  The subscriptions are not expensive.

**Useful Study Potential That I Recommend**.  Taken from http://www.moneyshow.com "Oliver L. Velez, founder of iFundTraders, LLC, international bestselling author, trader, advisor, and entrepreneur, is one of the most sought after speakers and teachers on the subject of trading financial markets for a living. His seminars and speaking events have been attended by traders all over the world, and his best selling books, Strategies for Profiting on Every Trade and Tools and Tactics...: http://www.fool.com : The Motley Fool, for additional fundamental information about companies worthy of potential investments.  http://finance.yahoo.com/market-overview: Site for

Company information of all types and uses. A must daily visit for market and company tracking.

**Must Books For Your Library**. Stan Weinstein's "Secrets for Profiting in Bull and Bear Markets" "Elliot Wave Principle" by Frost and Prechter. Anything by Toni Turner, President of TrendStar Group, Inc., is an accomplished technical analyst as well as a popular educator and sought-after speaker in the financial arena. She is the author of the best selling books: A Beginner's Guide to Day Trading Online, 2nd Ed., A Beginner's Guide to Short-term Trading, 2nd Ed., Short-Term Trading in the New Stock Market, and Invest to Win: Earn & Keep Profits in Bull..." "John Murphy, former technical analyst for CBNC, has more than 40 years of market experience. He is the author of several best selling books including, Technical Analysis of the Financial Markets. Mr. Murphy was given the first award by the International Federation of Technical Analysts for outstanding contribution to global technical analysis and has received the Market Technician's Annual Award...." Read information that you want to learn more about and that you think will help you improve your skills.

# Chapter One: Indicators and their use in every day trading.

## Indicators and Their Use in Every Day Investing.
First I open the chart to the company I want to study. I keep all the company charts in categories. The ones in which I own equities are the Visual Trades category. Daily I look at each chart to decide, if I need to dump it, or take profits, or let it ride. After each stock has been carefully studied I mark the ones that need to be sold, the ones where additional shares need to be purchased, or the ones I will hold until tomorrow. I will do my trading at about 2 pm before the market closes.

The portfolio charts are available for daily viewing and are updated each trading day.

For example: One of the stocks I currently own is EXTR (Extreme Networks, Inc.), it is a low priced stock that trades on the NASDAQ but has the potential to rise exponentially. On the day after Christmas in twenty thirteen I will upgrade this chart daily and post it to my web site.

All of my indicators are holding steady with a couple off positive slightly. I will explain the entire process in a step by step process starting at the top of the chart. But first, I chose this stock for an example because I want to stress several points. 1: hold your trade until your information tells you to strike:. 2. There is always the possibility for error so be ready to bail: 3: do not expect to get rich quick with this method. You are trading with a limited amount of capital, using strict investment principles, and you have to limit for the number of shares you can purchase.

I am buying 45 shares for near $324.25 which is slightly more than ten percent of my trading account allotted amount. I try not to exceed more than 20% of my trading account. Each trade costs seven dollars to exercise and that becomes a large percentage of a small share investment. The sell is also seven dollars so the expense makes the need to be correct imperative. When I trade several times a month, with a much larger investment capital, I use TradeStation because I can make one hundred trades for zero cost with a one dollar commission for each trade up to one hundred shares. Scottrade ® is my choice in this instance because it is so user friendly and about as inexpensive as you will find. With that platform I can trade with a minimum of expense. In the old days a small investor was doomed to limited trades because of the exorbitant costs of having to do business through a full service brokerage firm.

Click this URL --> EXTR Once you have the chart then simultaneously view this book and the EXTR chart. With the two screens viewed together we can talk about what you see. Once you have both windows open then just follow this text. This chart in the first window is as it is viewed in my membership cloud At Stockcharts.com. ® My trading platform is Scottrade ® but their charting platform is not as graphic as that on the StockCharts site.

For many years I have subscribed to StockCharts.com ® and it has become a quick and easy tool for me.  My reasoning for using it is that the graphic tools make maintaining my web site very easy.  I can apply the visual attributes necessary to explain each chart's condition immediately.  Your chart graphic presentation is the entire chart area with a supporting Chart Attributes section for setting the parameters of each indicator.  I will demonstrate the ones I use as we progress through the presentation.

December Twenty-Sixth, Twenty Thirteen:  This is the chart I worked with on the day of this writing.  Starting at the top I will explain what I use regularly, and to what extent, I believe it helps in my trade selections. I bought this stock on October tenth, twenty thirteen.  I had sold it earlier for a small profit because it was losing impetus and not trading in a large enough Average True Range (ATR).

Also, some of the other indicators were negative.  When I repurchased the stock there was change in the indicators to the positive side.  At this time the price trend appears to be in a full blown Weinstein's stage 2.  If this is happening then I will be adding stock to my portfolio.  If I do purchase additional shares you will see it reflected in the historical pricing date and current price block which today is green.  I am trading this equity because I subscribe to "the WSD Insider".  It is not necessary for you to subscribe to this service.  The publication alone is not very expensive and is educational for anyone who is dedicated to trading.  Most of the other services they offer are prohibitive in cost and, in my opinion, they do not give me anything I can't duplicate by using my own trading technique.  I am a subscriber because the in depth study they do to investigating a company's fundamental strength is unequaled.  They can interview and communicate with all kinds of company officials.  Their detailed inquiries about the financial and operational strengths provide valuable company insight.  With the WSD" input I have decided to follow this company until its potential dissipates.

There are people who do quite well at trading by not working this hard but they have other rules and methods that help them make money. These are methods I have adapted which suit my investing style. Years of study and application have made them trustworthy in my employ and I apply them to keep me profitable. There are also the individuals that say, "all of this means nothing; that all you have to do is to pay them to show you how to get rich working just ten minutes or so a day and do what they say." They also may make money (I doubt it). They make their money if you buy their hype. I trust and apply what I prescribe. These are methods that I have picked up over the years and I trust them to keep me profitable.

# Chapter Two: Actual chart information and explanation.

The chart to the below is as EXTR appeared on 12/26/2013. I use this file to track my trade. If you have downloaded the entire file you will see that an Attributes section makes the chart file appear much longer. It is this bottom section that projects the story of price tends. If you have downloaded the StockCharts.com ® chart for EXTR You can then see the full extent of the image.

The blocks of text explain what I have found by researching other sites and documents to get a better picture of the strength of EXTR. All of the other documentation is basically produced in the chart proximity and is directly part of the story of market progression.

**Actual Chart Information**

Starting at the top I will explain everything I use and to what extent I believe it helps in my trade selections. I sold this stock on July 31 for a small profit because it was losing impetus and not trading in a large enough Average True Range.

To see all charts clearly:
- Go to the stockcharts.com home page
- Click on link to the right Below Links "Public Charts List"
- Then scroll all the way to the bottom and click "Show Me All Public ChartsLists
- Hold Ctrl F to open a search and then
- Search for Don Markham and click that link, here you can see all charts clearly.

(ATR) plus some of the other indicators were negative. I repurchased the stock on 10/25/2013 because of a change in the indicators. Also, it appears that EXTR is in a full blown Weinstein's stage 2. Hope for a long run and a good profit.

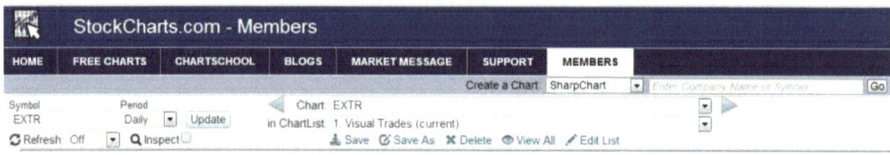

At the very top of the chart graphic is the stock symbol that has been selected (EXTR). If you click the down button you can view all of the charts listed in that file, (Visual Trades (current). Just below the Chart area is the selection marked as Symbol, and Period. Selecting the Daily block arrow shows a menu with all of the time periods you can select for the duration of the price range. This particular chart is a Daily period. Meaning that each candle on the chart is for the trading of each daily period. If I want to view a weekly time period I get a single candle for each week, showing me the price range in that weekly period. The selections in this instance gives you the opportunity to pick a time period as short as one minute. The Update block makes the chart current.

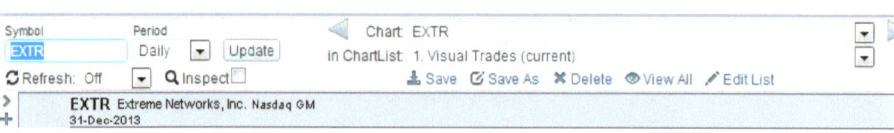

Top left graphic section of the next chart portion. To see this entire section visualize the top right section as an extension of the above.

The heading designating this chart is EXTR. Directly following it is the title with the full company name (Extreme Networks, Inc. NASDAQ in this case. Immediately below that is listed the last date this particular chart is active .here it is 26-Dec-2013. I always check this to make sure the stock is trading on the right date because some companies (including this one) will not start trading immediately at the opening bell.

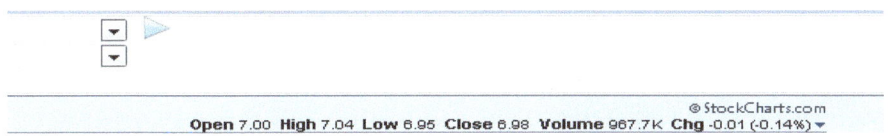

Follow across the page to the area that says open, followed by a number, High (followed by a number. Low followed by a number, and close followed by a number. I like last to replace the close because during the trading period that is what this indicates. I watch this area closely because it tells me exactly how the stock is trading. I used to draw arrows from these areas to the candle price. Now I draw colored lines under the open, high, low, close areas on the price candles. The open has a black line where it occurred, the High is underlined in blue, and the low is underlined in red and the last or close is green. I have learned to be more aware of what a stock is doing by watching the story told by the candles. I first got interested in this detail from an Oliver Velez seminar given at a Las Vegas Money Show meeting. I will explain how I use this information when I get to the candle price area. If you have questions just go to the Chart School on the main menu and search.

# Chapter Three: The Chart's main graphic section.

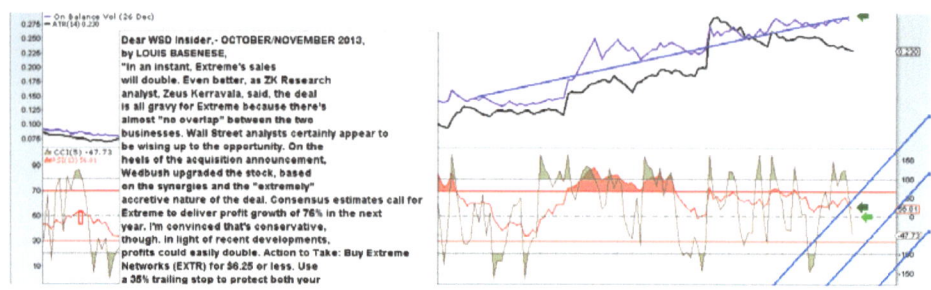

Above note the small text indicating the indicators On Balance Volume (OBV) as well as Average True Range (ATR), the information behind it in parentheses are its settings. You can see how these are drawn by scrolling down to the area designated Chart Attributes, and on down to the Indicator section. Definitions of indicators can be found in the Chart School area of Stockcharts.com ® or Wikepedia. The OBV indicator has a blue line drawn to represent its trend at the end of the line is a positive green arrow. The more green arrows you see on the chart, the stronger is the stock. OBV is, over time, from mid-August to today a strong positive. I will explain the price candles later but if you scroll to them now you will note that their trend is also up. The large white text box is the information provided by WSD Insider and is there to keep me posted about the fundamental side of the stock. This stock also contains another of these text blocks.

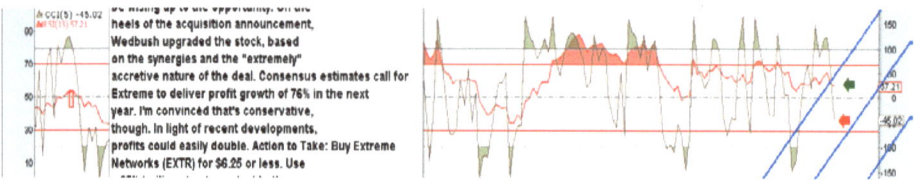

The next block on the chart is marked CCI and RSI with their settings following them. CCI or Commodity Channel Index is my favorite indicator because it moves so rapidly. It gives you a trend change very quickly. I believe that if it is above the 0 line, and moving up that the stock is good to go. If it crosses the 0 line down I am usually out, or thinking about shorting the stock. The Relative Strength Index (RSI), is a similar indicator but it is much slower. I don't feel like it is as quickly correct as the CCI. I bought this stock when both the RSI and CCI were above the 0 line. In fact the CCI was in overbought territory and the RSI was just crossing. To me overbought territory is sometimes the best time to buy. There were other indicators still saying no, but I will show you what I saw and why I decided to pull the trigger.

This next block is the heart of the chart. It is where the action is. Everything else just amplifies and magnifies this block. I call it the price trend block. There are several indicators in this block also. I think the most important are the candles. Ordinarily I don't look for individual nomenclature like Hanging Man, Hammers, Morning Stars, etc. I deem them important and will give them my attention but primarily I look for size and movement. As I mentioned earlier, Oliver Velez gave me my take on candles. His premise is that size, if large and solid, will indicate direction of price. He thinks that the daily candle growth will give you direction and momentum. Let's take a look at the chart.

Back up to where you see the **Open**, **High**, **Low** and **close (last)** label graphic display. This part of candle study is hard to figure out at first but if you go through several candles you can understand it. The last candle has four lines drawn at different levels of the candle. Arrow (black) goes to the candle's opening. On Dec. 27 the opening price was $7.05 and there is a black line at that position on the candle. The high was at $7.15 and, as indicated by the blue line at that position. The low was underlined in red at the $6.95 position at the very bottom of the candle tail. The close or last underlined with green at $6.98. Here is what I know, once the candle was green from opening to high. It couldn't have opened and gone down because then the candle would have been red. It went up so its high was at the very top and it had to be a green candle. That would have been good. Instead it dropped all the way down to the red line (low) and moved up to its current place. We'll look again at 2pm. At 2pm the chart opened went up and then went down and closed close to its open. There was almost no change from open until close. This was a spinning top and no indicator for action.

At that point the bears have and will hold it unless the price rises to $7or above. Also, Velez says that if candle price is way above the daily moving averages that the price is likely to correct enough to drive you out of the trade.

Beneath the price candles are three moving average lines named the **Daily Moving Averages** (DMAs). They are indicated on my charts by three different lines. You can see them labeled in the far right green area. First is the stock symbol, then the Moving Average (MA) 20. The 20 designates it as a 20 DMA and it appears on the chart as a dotted blue line. Next is a red MA (30) appearing on the chart as a red solid line. There is another red solid line that represents the 200 DMA. All of the DMAs need to be below the price line to be positive. Here, price is approaching the 30 DMA, which is not good.

From Chart School: "**Volume by Price** is an indicator that shows the amount of volume for a particular price range. Volume by Price bars are shown horizontal on the left side of the chart to match up with price points. These color-coded bars divide volume based on up periods (green) and volume on down periods (red). Chartists can use Volume by Price to identify high volume price points that may provide support or resistance."

My primary use for this indicator is to find a support and a resistance area. The graphic bars are shown on the chart for information purposes but usually I just show the resistance and support bars that are located by the position of Volume by Price. Support is the lowest bar that marks a price low area and resistance is marked where the price has traded at its highest point within the upper bar. Note that price tried to break resistance but never quite achieved the feat. If it accomplishes a break above resistance than resistance can becomes support and stage 2 continues. This factor will hold me in this trade until it hits my stop loss range around $6.75.

I have the **volume** set on the bottom of the price chart. This is not given near the attention that it deserves, even from me. I learned about volume by studying Toni Turner's Short Term Trading in the New Stock Market book. Pages 153 and 154 and all the rest of the book.

# Chapter Four: *The lower Indicator section.*

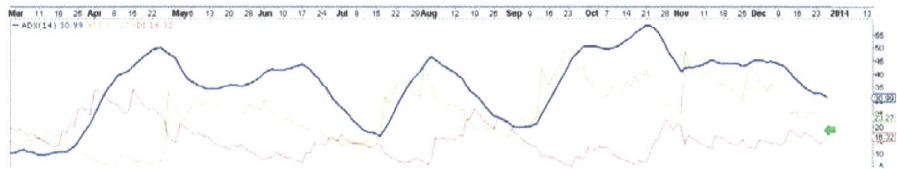

### Average Directional Index (ADX)   <-- URL

I basically just want to know that the green line is above the red line for this index to be positive. When it is reflecting a green line below the red line, then I am not participating.

TRIX is a momentum oscillator that displays the percent rate of change of a triple exponentially smoothed moving average. It was developed in the early 1980's by Jack Hutson, an editor for Technical Analysis of Stocks and Commodities magazine.

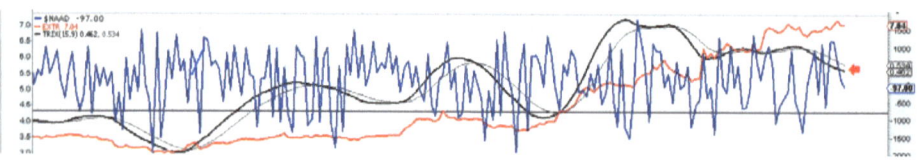

I track TRIX with the market that brokers the stock, here it is the NASDAQ. I like the dark black line to be over the light black line. In EXTR it is negative (noted by the red arrow) and that is not good.

MACD turns two trend-following indicators, <u>moving averages</u>, into a momentum oscillator by subtracting the longer moving average from the shorter moving average. As a result, the MACD offers the best of both worlds: **trend following and momentum.**

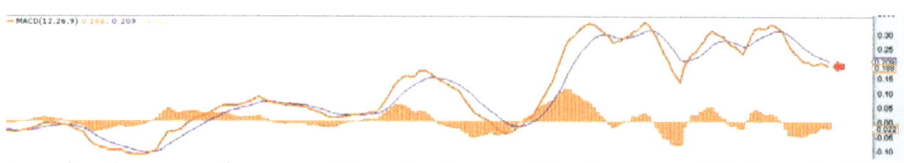

I again place a red arrow where the brown line is crossed below the blue line. And if the Stochastic (next indicator) is red, I am close to being out of the trade. In this instance both are negative and I'm nervous.

The Stochastic Oscillator is a momentum indicator that shows the location of the close relative to the high-low range over a set number of periods. According to an interview with Lane, the Stochastic Oscillator "doesn't follow price, it doesn't follow volume or anything like that. It follows the speed or the momentum of price. As a rule, the momentum changes direction before price." As such, bullish and bearish divergences in the Stochastic Oscillator can be used to foreshadow reversals.

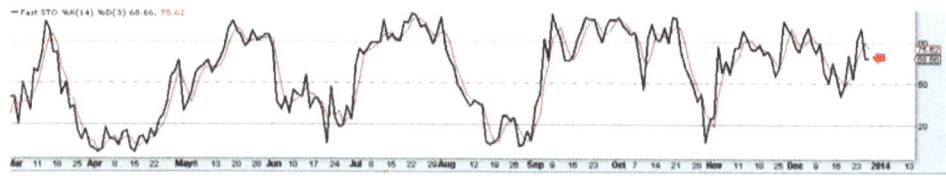

When this one and the MACD agree I get very antsy. EXTR better not follow its current path very long or I am gone. I will set my stop loss very close to the current price.

## Intricate Chart Manipulation

This menu starts with **annotate (flash) (java)** which allows you to work on the chart by manipulating all of the whistles and bells. You can draw lines, rectangles, and circles. You can make all of your additions most any color and size. You can make them take the direction you want them to go. You can write text or use symbols and do your own art. You can make that chart tell its story the way you want it told. I believe that a picture can improve the data it enhances. Practice with it and you will succeed in telling yourself a better story.

**Print:** use it if you need your product in hard copy.

**Share:** Self explanatory

**Linkable Version** - select this area and a URL block appears and you can copy it almost anywhere. Copy it to your web site and when you select the symbol the entire chart file appears where it was copied as a URL.

Past Data is helpful if you are tracking a specific time period for price or volume. One of the methods I am testing uses the stock float Analysis which using time exposed during a total float turnover initiated by .W. D. Gann. He thought that float turnover information was important and supposedly made his fortune following the concept. I am still studying to understand how it is applied and am not very close to the answer. I purchase a W.D. Gann book titled Treasure Discovered but it didn't answer the float question. I have just ordered another book by Steve Woods titled Float Analysis: Powerful Technical Indicators Using Price and Volume. In It Gann is credited with originating the concept. Maybe this book will give me the information I need to enhance my research.

**Instructions and Report Problems:** I never use these but if you need them don't hesitate.

**ChartStyles:** This transforms a regular chart file into the style that you have created. The style you see on my charts is called solid ChartStyle. I have other styles that I use and I even alter the styles from time to time. When I discover different data that I want to make a permanent part of my charts, then I change the style to reflect that data.

# Chapter Five: The Chart Attributes Section
### Chart Attributes:

This is a difficult section to explain and teach. I will briefly explain some of the parts that I use and include one detailed addition to a chart file.

In the bar marked **Periods** the menu block is set for Daily.  Under **Range** the block contains Predefined Range.  Under **Years** it's 0.  Under **Months** It's 10.  And under Days it's 0.  I want my chart to have additional space at the end of the page so I have entered 10 in the **Extra** Bars area moving down to the **Type** heading and the selection block below has a down arrow which allows several choices and I have selected  Candlesticks.  Under **Size** I have selected 1280.  Below **Color Scheme** the selection is Murphy.  You can follow the remaining categories as they appear in the chart.  You can explore every possibility to understand the many qualities of these selections.

This is the section of the book where I will give an example of the power of Chart Attributes.  It is a combination that I have named **the Power Pop.**  This is an occurrence where I require a price line to become complete before I will pull the trigger on a trade.  The first entry is located under the type heading which currently is Candlesticks.  Change Candlesticks to EquiVolume.  This changes the price area from Candlesticks to an EquiVolume area and gives you an idea of the strength by volume and price of the candle sequence.  This information allows me a better idea of the second part of the Power Pop.

A power Pop is initiated when the 20 DMA crosses and moves above the 30 DMA.  At this Point the DMA's do not have to be below the price line.  As the days pass I look for a wide long green block or several smaller green blocks moving above the chart's price line.  It occurred for EXTR on September 23.  At that point there was no negative indicators and I pulled the trigger.  It is still in a Weinstein stage 2 but weakening some, but I won't dump until my stop is reached.  Or there is a reverse Power Pop.

The Power Pop is a combination of several pieces of data and does indicate stock trend.  All of the chart data should be incorporated into your decision making before you complete a trade.  The Power Pop begins the motion but everything else drives it.  Be sure all of your research agrees for a positive result.

Experiment with this section if you don't already know about its power. If you can or have mastered this aspect of technical trading then you are way ahead of me and this book. If you are not a master then I challenge you to do it. I will barely scratch the surface the rest is up to you.

# Chapter Six: The Dow Theory

**The Dow Theory**

From Wikipedia, the free encyclopedia: "The Dow theory on stock price movement is a form of technical analysis that includes some aspects of sector rotation. The theory was derived from 255 Wall Street Journal editorials written by Charles H. Dow (1851–1902), journalist, founder and first editor of the Wall Street Journal and co-founder of Dow Jones and Company. Following Dow's death, William Peter Hamilton, Robert Rhea and E. George Schaefer organized and collectively represented Dow Theory, based on Dow's editorials. Dow himself never used the term Dow Theory nor presented it as a trading system."
Visit this site and study the entire article if you want to know about a terrific theory that is still pertinent.

I believe in this concept so thoroughly that I routinely maintain a weekly up dated chart for my clients. The 27 December chart is pictured below on the next page.

**A Personal Story and One Reason I'm Interested in CLNE**

Another factor that excites me is the inter relatedness of the two components of the theory. The DJIA and TRAN (transportation). John Murphy the master mind behind stockcharts.com theorized and then through, extensive research, proved his theory to the satisfaction of most traders. That not just world stock markets but all markets are interrelated. So, as Charles Dow wrote, transportation drives the Dow. Other things help but transportation is the big dog chasing, which seems to help the DJIA trend.

The theory quoted from Wikipedia, "The theory was derived from 255 Wall Street Journal editorials written by journalist, founder and first editor of the Wall Street Journal and co-founder of Dow Jones and Company." I (I day, and the day following, which would be a Sunday or a holiday, to check and update my version of the tren reasoning behind the theory and the creativity of the man who postulated it. To find out more go to the URL a Another factor that excites me is the inter relatedness between the two components of the theory. The DJIA a Murphy the master mind behind stockcharts.com theorized and then through extensive research, proved his

**12/21: It has been an unbelievable market for the past few months. By watching The**, 'Transp
**Dow Theory you could tell that our money people knew that things were not dire just grevious. Friday, 13 was some relief from the down trend. Now we have to wory about lower lows and lower highs. Higher highs and Higher highs are very good because it continues a bull trend. I can't predict but I can certainly follow my research. It is not looking good but it beets the alternative of being all bad. CCI came back a little but is still negative. RSI is also negative. Daily Moving Averages (DMAs) are positive but above the price line which is not good. ADX, TRIX, MACD and Stochistics are giving negaative information. But, look at $Trans 9Transportation), Just Trucking and hauling right on up. 12/21: more of the good stuff. Looking for a new high high.**

09/18 almost got a lower low but then it took off.. All good news.

1000 drop in 28 days

## Some of My Former Postings:

I will post the newest research on the Dow Theory first. Then, to view a few previous posts, select my daily edits. I will list a few older posts here. If anyone would like the older post, not listed, check the site. 10/15: This is very exciting. We are in the midst of a threatened shut down and the market has just missed another lower low and is headed in an up trend. Today the 15$^{th}$ we are down about 50 points after an up week. The momentum may be shifting but we'll see. Hope for some good news from the government. The politicians remind me of a game my cousin and I used to play called did too, did not: can too, can not: will too, will not: are too, am not: etc. Childish isn't it.

10/25: This is very exciting. We are in just passed a threatened shut down and the market is just in a good up trend. Today the 25th we are looking toward another higher high. The momentum doesn't appear to be slowing. The politicians do not seem to be scaring the Markets. Especially the Dow.

12/15: It has been an unbelievable market for the past few months. By watching The Dow Theory you could tell that our money people knew that things were not dire just grievous. Friday, 13 was some relief from the down trend. Now we have to worry about lower lows and lower highs. Higher highs and higher highs are very good because it continues a bull trend. I can't predict but I can certainly follow my research. It is not looking good but it beats the alternative of being all bad. CCI came back a little but is still negative. RSI is also negative. Daily Moving Averages (DMAs) are positive but above the price line which is not good ADX. TRIX. MACD and Stochastics are giving negative information. But, look at $Trans (Transportation), Just Trucking and hauling right on up. Maybe Christmas Week will be more of the good stuff.

12/15 -12/21: It has been an unbelievable market for the past few months. By watching The Dow Theory you could tell that our money people knew that things were not dire just grievous. Friday, 13 was some relief from the down trend. Now we have to worry about lower lows and lower highs. Higher highs and higher highs are very good because it continues a bull trend. I can't predict but I can certainly follow my research. It is not looking good but it beets the alternative of being all bad. CCI came back a little but is still negative. RSI is also negative. Daily Moving Averages (DMAs) are positive but above the price line which is not good, ADX. TRIX. MACD and Stochastics are giving negative information. But, look at $Trans 9Transportation), Just Trucking and hauling right on up. 12/21: more of the good stuff. Looking for a new higher high.

12/27: Unbelievable still but DMA's are closing and price is well above them which is a negative. Stochastics is also turning to negative but all else looks good. May be the red dogi is nothing but a hiccup.

## Chapter Seven: Thoughts and Ramblings

In 1950 (that's 62 years ago) when I was in high school, my father (dad to me) farmed nearly 3 sections of land. We owned many gas powered vehicles. One of those vehicles was a Dodge truck and it was a pain to get started. The engine had to be almost perfectly tuned for it to operate properly. A high school buddy of mine was the son of a blacksmith-mechanic so I talked dad into going to "Jake" (the friend's father) for help. I don't know how hard the battle was for "Jake" but he talked dad into converting that old Dodge to propane gas (what we called it). Bingo. In a short period of time every gasoline powered piece of equipment, including our personal autos were propane powered. Here is the "rest of the story"; oil changes required only one quart of oil plus the filter. The one quart was to replace what was lost with the filter change. Tune ups were almost never needed (also a big saving), and the fuel was cheaper because back then the tax was much less. He ran natural gas in his vehicles until he died in 2000. I'm betting on Boon and CLNE.

# Chapter 8: Follow Up Information

### Six Days of Trading After January 2014:

The Jan 2 chart is on the next page is an image necessary as a tool in the learning process. It is about following your research in order to be current with every trade. I do this with every stock I own and some that I am just following. If possible you should place the text where you can read it and view the chart simultaneously. The chart is in trading day number six. Look at the vertical red line that extends from the chart top to the bottom, covering the price and continuing down the entire left side of the chart image. This chart has a red, a green and another red. It was necessary to show additional days in order for you to see the arrows. As we work forward you will get a better idea of the process, how it looks and how to understand the data. Read the indicator information in the book.

January 2: The day's price opened at $7.06, its low was $6.86 and the high was $6.99. That was the red candle's total day's movement. That move reflected a loss of seven cents. I was getting a little nervous because some of the indicators were negative. My stop loss is at $6.75. Follow the green arrows shown on the edge of the image. All of the arrows we are viewing will be on the right edge of the image. The first one is at the upper right and points to the On Balance Volume (OBV). It is green because the blue line under OBV is slanted up and that is a positive sign. Drop all the way down to the next green arrow and see that it is pointing to a wavy red line. That is the Relative Strength Index (RSI) The RSI is above the 0 line so it is positive. The next arrow is red and it is pointed to a wildly up and down blue line and that is the Commodity Channel Index (CCI). It is so far under the 0 line that it is in what is known as over sold territory. Way negative for my taste. Next is the price line and I have two green arrows to explain it. The first is to show that the price is above the Daily Moving Averages (DMAs). The next proclaims that the DMAs are separated and positive.

While we are in the area I would like to say what that resistance line is all about. I have seen the price get very close to breaking resistance, so I am ready to double down if it does. All indicators have to be positive, or something else occur to offset a negative, before I move especially the way things are moving now.

Go all the way down below the support line and the volume area until you can see a green line above a red line. That is the Average Directional Index (ADX). As long as the green line is above the red it is positive. The distance is important and with practice you can understand it better. Next is the TRIX indicator and I use it in conjunction with the $NAAD which is the symbol for the NASDAQ. The reason I do this is because it is helpful to combine the TRIX with the market where the stock is traded. This is negative because the TRIX line is below the NAAD. Next is the MACD and that is also negative and a reason to join with the CCI and be ready to sell. The last block is Fast Stochastics (STO).  This one is like CCI and becomes negative and positive quickly.  Today there is a blue arrow pointing to its position and that is a symbol I use to show no decision of negative or positive.

I use a subscription source to keep me informed about how a particular company may be doing its business.  They are very good with their research because they actually visit different businesses, their leadership, behind the scenes manipulations and the balance sheet.  These are things I do not have the clout or the expertise to accomplish.  I will follow with a small piece of the text in the box on the chart to demonstrate.

OCTOBER/NOVEMBER 2013 -by LOUIS BASENESE - "Founded in 1996, Extreme is a leading provider of network infrastructure quote from WSD Insider, "...equipment, including high-performance Ethernet switches. How does Extreme keep up with the big boys? First of all, the company offers an open-source, scalable platform..."

**EXTR** Extreme Networks, Inc. Nasdaq GM
10-Jan-2014

Open 7.37 High 7.53 Low 7.32 Close 7.44 Volume 1.2M

**OCTOBER/NOVEMBER 2013** by LOUIS BASENESE - "Founded in 1996, Extreme is a leading provider of network infrastructure quote from WSD Insider, "...equipment, including high performance ethernet switches.

How does Extreme keep up with the big boys? First of all, the company offers an open source, scalable platform. Its products work across multiple networks and service provider platforms, instead of being part of a single source, highly proprietary solution. Such flexibility naturally makes gaining market share easier. Second ? and most importantly ? the company is a consummate innovator." Consensus estimates call for Extreme to deliver profit growth of 76% in the next year. I'm convinced that's conservative, though. In light of recent developments, profits could easily double.
Either way, share prices promise to respond strongly to the upside.
Add it all up, and it's time we target the epicenters of growth in the market and position our portfolios for "extreme" profits. Action to Take: Buy Extreme Networks (EXTR) for $6.25 or less. Use a 35% trailing stop to protect both your principal and profits. Limit your position size to no more than 1% of your total portfolio. WSD EXTREME PROFITS AHEAD!LET'S ROUND OUT THE INVESTMENT CASE WITH THREE

**KILLER FUNDAMENTALS... Solid backlog growth:** Over the last year, Extreme's backlog grew over 50% to top $16 million. Granted, that's only equal to about 5% of annual sales. Nevertheless, the growth indicates that demand for Extreme's products is moving solidly in the right direction.
Enviable institutional ownership:
Extreme Networks is up over 20% since October. Is it still a good "Buy" at current prices? - J.R.

| Symbol | Open Date | Open Price | Current Price | Percentage Gain | Recommend |
|---|---|---|---|---|---|
| EXTR | 10/17/2013 | $5.66 | $6.95 | 22.79% | buy |

12/10/2013 EXTR BOUGHT 45 SHARES $7.0499 $324.25)
12/17 - $23 @ 6.68
12/30 - $17 @ 6.99 some negatives appearing
1/9 - +$5 @ 7.43

Up 3% for 2013

Resistance
stop
support

Dear WSD Insider,- OCTOBER/NOVEMBER 2013,
by LOUIS BASENESE,
"In an instant, Extreme's sales
will double. Even better, as ZK Research
analyst, Zeus Kerravala, said, the deal
is all gravy for Extreme because there's
almost "no overlap" between the two
businesses. Wall Street analysts certainly appear to
be wising up to the opportunity. On the
heels of the acquisition announcement,
Wedbush upgraded the stock, based
on the synergies and the "extremely"
accretive nature of the deal. Consensus estimates call for
Extreme to deliver profit growth of 76% in the next
year. I'm convinced that's conservative,
though. In light of recent developments,
profits could easily double. Action to Take: Buy Extreme
Networks (EXTR) for $6.25 or less. Use
a 35% trailing stop to protect both your
principal and profits. Limit your position
size to no more than 1% of your total
portfolio."

The chart for this text is on next page and again try to get text and chart side by side. Understand that only the horizontal lines at the end of the charts are necessary for this and the remaining charts.

Trading day 2: Fri 01-03-2014 -Price opened at $6.99, its high was $7.07, with a low of $6.82, and a close at $7.03. A green candle day with a four cent gain. Average True Range (ATR) says it should move one way or the other by twenty three cents. We didn't make that by nineteen cents.

The same 3 indicators are negative and CCI has joined them. Not much changed drastically so I'm holding my position. But note that the DMAs are moving closer together. If this continues I will be on my toes for a negative move in price.

I am still not a happy trader with this stock. CCI is the one indicator that makes quick large moves and gives me an early alert when it goes from positive to negative.

I keep a text block on my charts with the day of the purchase and then entries showing where the price was on other days. Often I will delete every entry except the purchase and have only the last entry. I do not do this often. If I do, it means that I am probably ready to trade it because it is not making it's OBV for extended periods. Usually I keep additional dates and information in the block. Here the first entry is, 12/10/2013 EXTR BOUGHT 45 SHARES $7.0499 - total $324.25, next entry was 12/12 =-$23 @ 6.68 (this indicates that the stock was in the negative on that day by $23 loss). The last entry read: 12/30 =-$12 @ 6.99 some negatives appearing, and finally 1/9 =+$1 @ 7.32.

Here is another quote that is in a text block on the chart. OCTOBER/NOVEMBER 2013,by LOUIS BASENESE, "In an instant, Extreme's sales will double. Even better, as ZK Research analyst, Zeus Kerravala, said, the deal is all gravy for Extreme because there's almost "no overlap" between the two businesses. Wall Street analysts certainly appear to be wising up to the opportunity. On the heels of the acquisition announcement, Wedbush upgraded the stock, based on the synergies and the "extremely" accretive nature of the deal. Consensus estimates call for Extreme to deliver profit growth of 76% in the next year. I'm convinced that's conservative, though. In light of recent developments, profits could easily double. Action to Take: Buy Extreme Networks (EXTR) for $6.25 or less. Use a 35% trailing stop to protect both your principal and profits. Limit your position size to no more than 1% of your total portfolio.

| Symbol | Open Date | Open Price | Current Price | Percentage Gain | Recommend |
|--------|-----------|------------|---------------|-----------------|-----------|
| EXTR   | 10/17/2013 | $5.66     | $6.95         | 22.79%          | buy       |

Well they haven't doubled yet but they are still worth owning.

Note that the price and vertical lines are becoming easier to understand and that issue will continue to get easier, better to see and understand. It helps if you study and work some each day on your research and trading skills.  I have been at this since 1987.  I have three degrees and sometimes I think I am not going to ever get to the expert level. Hopefully your expertise is in math and economics because that makes it much easier for you to see the circumstances involved in trading equities.  Below is a view of just the price area and the line is just before our current text. The full chart follows on the next page.

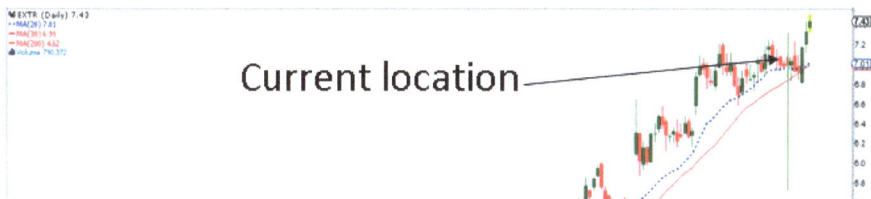
Current location

The final series will show the complete pictures of the charts from the first page to Fri 01-10-2014 the ending date at the writing of this book.

Find the third horizontal line which is red for the next day of trading. Trading day Mon. 01-06-2014    Price opened at $7.08, with a high of $7.23, a low of $6.93 and a close of $6.93.  This became a down day with a loss of fifteen cents.  Still not a day that met the ATR.  It was a larger movement in price then the previous trading day but thankfully not up to its standard.

This is a period when I want to look at my stop loss because it could be going into a Weinstein's stage three consolidation.  If you haven't read his book yet, do so. The third stage is a forerunner to what is usually a steep correction.  Now the CCI and the RSI are both above the 0 line so I am not bailing yet.  The DMAs are almost touching and I'm still in a nervous state of mind.  The bottom three indicators are still holding negative.

Now is the time to reflect and prepare.  I have a good sized red candle and the candle guru says that if one day has a large, basically marubozu candle then the very next trading period has a 95% chance of being red also.  Wait until the next day and see what happens.  But stay alert for the worst case scenario.

I am thinking about moving my stop loss up to limit losses of any magnitude.

Because the text used so little space I will just show the price portion of the chart because the indicator portion is basically the same.

The predicted red candle appeared. It didn't thrill me but I expected it. Tue 01-07-2014 began the day at $6.98, went to $7.09, then dropped to $6.84 and finished at $6.93. It did not come close to trading at the ATR standard. I didn't get too upset and I didn't feel like it was a deep correction. The indicators were changed slightly for the better. Below is the Chart graphics for this text.

Wed 01-08-2014 it opened at $6.82, the high hit $7.17, the low was the opening at $6.82 and the close was the high $7.17. The marubozu candle was large and green, meaning that tomorrow's should also be up. I'm good with that.

The indicators got a lot better and we finally got a decent ATR. Price gained twenty five cents, a full quarter. CCI got positive and so did STO. The charts trading text block was getting close to positive again. Just wait on that next green candle. The DMAs almost touched. But I didn't worry because things were looking up, and I quit worrying about my stop loss. I couldn't wait for tomorrow's arrival.

Again we will only post a price chart portion.

Chart to follow. The market opened with everything in my portfolio up except KOL which I will dump even though the stop loss is lower. Thu 01-09-2014: The market opened at 7.20, went to $7.43, fell to $7.15 and closed at $7.28 with the gain of eight cents. But a green arrow as predicted. What happened to the indicators is positive. CCI skyrocketed into overbought territory and I enjoyed the graphic. Overbought is not bad just a term used for the upper range territory. There was another large green candle that lost close to 50% of its gain.

That according to Oscar does not predict a gain for tomorrow. If that 20 DMA can separate a tad more, it will form what I call a kiss and tell. And that will be all good. The last 3 are gaining on a positive indication. We'll see what tomorrow's surprise will be.

I will put the entire chart below.

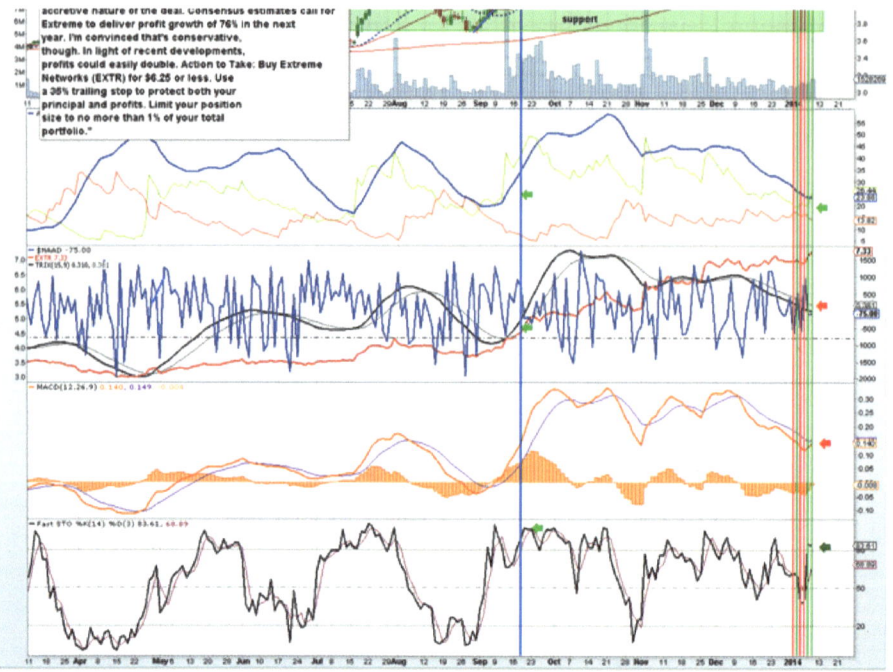

Fri 01-10-2014: This is a down NASDAQ $7.50 at the current time and here is EXTR up. It opened at $7.37, with a high of $7.49, then down to $7.32 and at the close it was $7.44. It was is a seven cent raise on a down market day. Saying that is pretty strong is putting it mildly. The other thing that I might point out is the 20 and 30 DMAs. They came together like they were going to cross and then the blue separated and turned slightly up. I call that a Kiss and Tell. The tell part is to continue the upward trend. We will see if that is the case here. Only TRIX is negative. I am one day away from doubling down.

When we started this book project, I had held this stock with reluctance because it was moving so slowly and was looking as if it was in a stage three correction. Now it has the appearance of trending upward again. May be it is still in a strong stage two.

Just the upper chart follows because you can still view the full chart on the web site.

Full Chart No Attributes No Annotations Below

To see all charts clearly:
- Go to the stockcharts.com home page
- Click on link to the right Below Links "Public Charts List"
- Then scroll all the way to the bottom and click "Show Me All Public ChartsLists
- Hold Ctrl F to open a search and then
- Search for Don Markham and click that link, here you can see all charts clearly.

# Chapter 9: The Kiss and Tell Phenomenon

Reminisces from an earlier decade resulted in the discovery of this phenomenon. Clearly, trading was hard for me because of my lack of mathematic and economics skills. I understood that the market was an expert in mocking most of my efforts aimed at making good decisions. Any trading success required me to gain, apply, and profit from all the knowledge that I could find and absorb. Diligently I sought and studied everything I could, as the sports talking heads are always saying, get my mind around it. Years of investing, with some success, and fewer failures has brought me to a period where I am able to more consistently succeed.

Recently I saw a phenomenon that reminded me of an Eliot Wave concept I encountered in one of their publications. I don't remember exactly which document, nor do I want to spend the time looking up the details. I just know it was a concept outlined by one of their analysts. It used an indicator's two lines, which touched, but did not completely cross one another. He called it a "hook". I have named it the "Kiss and Tell". The 20 DMA kisses the 30 DMA, from above, but does not cross under it. I have come across the same action in reverse and I believe it may indicate a down trend. I have seen that same occurrence many times in my studies of Daily Moving Averages. Here are the results of that remembrance regarding that instance and my discovery of how it applies for my own use.

As most everyone is aware, I make detailed studies of the Daily Moving Averages of the stocks in my portfolios. I pay strict attention to their location and their relationship within their surroundings. I also watch their reactions with one another. Below is a chart of a specific detail showing some of the things that I want to illustrate concerning the Kiss and Tell phenomenon and DMA's.

This is the StockCharts.com 01/17/2014 Daily image of the price line for EXTR. This is the same version that I have been using throughout this book, it is just a little further along in time.

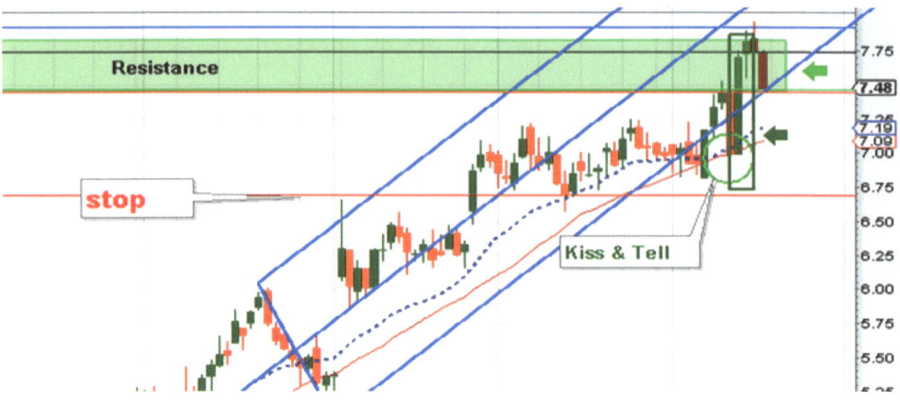

One of the indicators is the Pitch Fork (illustrated in blue). It is an overlay which I use in nearly all of my studies. The Pitch Fork can reinforce my attitude concerning the trend initiated with the "Kiss and Tell" piece of the puzzle.

The blue dotted line is the 20 DMA and the solid thin red line is the 30 DMA. The 20 just touched the 30 and continued its upward climb. The green circle highlights the "Kiss". This is the point I call the Kiss and Tell area. The "Tell" portion is the large green candle that is encompassed by the green rectangle. Should the 20 cross over the 30 and continue down then a trend change is probably happening. That is not occurring here and this fact increases my confidence in this trade. There is a third red line, not the horizontal red line near 6.75, but another one not visible on this image. It is the 200 DMA which occurs lower down on a full EXTR chart image.

There is a relationship between the price and the DMA. When the price gets too far above the 20 or 30 DMA then it is susceptible to a trend change. The methods I use for price research comes from Velez's productions, and he is the proprietor of the Price to DMA relationship theory.

The two larger green arrows place my attention on the positive nature of other aspects of the DMA positions. If it were negative the arrows would be red. The green arrow pointing to the DMA section shows the space between the two. The wider the space the better the upward movement. Follow the DMA lines backward and you can see that as the gap narrows the price dips. The further apart it gets the more the stock accrues value.

I am concerned any time there is a large price drop because of many factors. The main one, in this instance, refers to the progression of the price line. I have previously mentioned Stan Weinstein, and I can't emphasize enough, his influence on Market technical research.

EXTR could be in the upper stages of a Stage 2 or it could be anywhere between the interior and the upper area. My concern may not be real, but if this is the beginning of a Stage 3 consolidation, then we need to be out with some profit. The reference to any stage is not length but time. Usually the stages are clear cut but not related to one another by length. For instance, the Elliot Wave's third wave, is typically the longest and strongest, of the three upward waves. This has been a long "Weinstein" stage 2 and it has touched the resistance bar but did not break above. If it breaks that resistance line then resistance becomes the new support area. Again we can't be sure that a consolidation Stage 3 will not ensue.

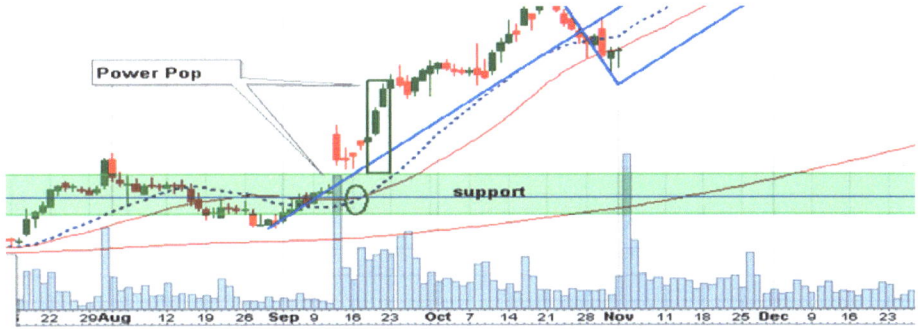

## The Power Pop Revisited

The Power Pop started just before price broke out of support. Bear with me in my regression but further insight into EXTR is now available. The green circle encompasses the area where the 20 DMA crossed above the 30 DMA. This is the "Power" and is almost always a sign of strength in the company. The first large green candle, inside the green rectangle, is the "Pop". It must follow closely after the DMA crosses. It is also the first move in what is probably a strong upward trend. In this case it hopefully begins a long "Weinstein Stage two".

The price tries to return to the pitchfork's central line. Once it attains the center line it will choose one of three actions. It will break out and trend upward, or it will form a consolidation along the center, or it will trend back downward. Here it has not achieved a break above but has started back down. This alarms me. However, I will not react just yet because the stock is profitable. One more red candle and it will have broken the fork's support and I will take the profit I have attained. I place the horizontal red line close to $6.75 in case there is a gap down. A gap down can happen instantly and should be addressed when it has reached a stopping point. Hopefully that point will not be below $6.75. As I stated above I will be exiting the trade at $7.45, if it reaches that point, on the next trading day.

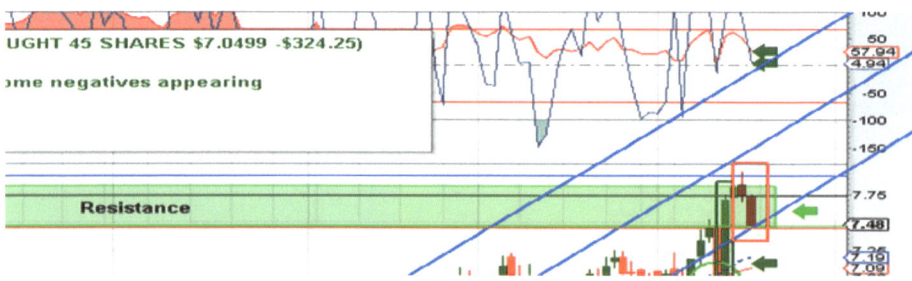

The top of the price line shows two red candle days. We have certainly made some hay while the run was on. I am not in the mood to lose that profit. One more red candle and I'll take my profit and run. I'm not expecting a stage 3 correction, but you never know because, "the market does what the market does".

I would be a happy trader if this was the end of red candles and resistance could be broken to the up side. Well time and the market will tell. If the run is over then we are not going to make much money on this trade, but I am confident that we will be able to reenter sometime in the near future.

May all your trade trends be positive and all your profits be monstrous.

# Chapter 10: How Hard Do You Want to Work?

I have read many authors who say, do not track too many stock. They may even recommend just two and at most three. I'm here to tell you to work hard if that is your desire. I segregate my charts by categories. Each category contains company charts that are listed by propinquity. The first category in my StockCharts.com cloud is titled "1. Visual Trades (current)." The list contains the stock of each company listed in my current portfolio. I also list here recent trades of any stock that has reached a point where my research tells me to sell; or that has been stopped out of a trade. This category is also closely tied to and can be viewed at my web page. In all, I have eleven categories holding from one in the "zz. Cisco" category, to eighteen in the "WSD All Portfolios" category.

Obviously I don't view all eleven categories daily. Some are only visited when it is necessary to study a company that has had the immediate reason for study. For instance, "zz. Cisco", has only one stock listed. You guessed it, Cisco. This one stock has cost me money in quantities that have been maddening. I blame it, not on my own faults, but on my feeling that it is manipulated by the large corporate traders. It seems that when I trade it the time has arisen to jerk it around. Recently it has appeared to have made a positive trend change with a "Power Pop". Had I purchased at the time of the occurrence I would have made a nice gain. Now it is above the DMA and with my Cisco track record I'm not in just yet. Like Cline I think it is a good company to track but I am remaining skeptical.

All indicators are telling me that this company can be purchase for $22.75 and could go to $26 but I am leery for several reasons. The first reason has to do with my track record concerning CSCO. I am also not sure that Stage 1 has run its course. If we wait for $24 we may still make a two dollar profit providing the indicators are with us. If the market holds and it does break above the blue square then I am in once again. If I trade it and it gaps down again then CSCO and I are through.

The largest category hosts eleven charts. This houses the portfolio of one of the services where I own an inexpensive subscription known as the "WSD Insider". I am testing their service because it is low in cost and is providing me what I need in terms of fundamental research. I have attempted to do my on fundamentals but I find I just can't get the inside information that an entity with a multitude of analysts to do the due diligence has. They also have another multitude to make the contacts necessary to know what the company is attempting to accomplish. If their information continues to be trusted then that is what I look at regularly.

I have tried other services but this one seems to be the least manipulative with their portfolios. I am listing this category with the companies that I am continually researching. This is a partial image taken from my StockCharts.com site and is not meant to relay anything except my stock symbol list.
If you are working with multiple charts and indicators. This site (in my opinion) is simply the best.

| Symbol | Name | Close | Chg | % Change | Sector | Industry | Date |
|---|---|---|---|---|---|---|---|
| ATX | ATX | 21.50 | -0.02 | -0.09% | Staples | Nondurable Home Products | 1-17 16 00 |
| CME | CME | 75.49 | -0.01 | -0.01% | Financial | Investment Services | 1-17 16 00 |
| CTHR | CTHR | 4.56 | -0.07 | -1.51% | Cyclicals | Clothing & Accessories | 1-17 16 00 |
| FARO | FARO - Inovators | 55.01 | -0.99 | -1.77% | Technology | Electronic Equipment | 1-17 16 00 |
| FEZ | FEZ tradinf portfolio | 41.72 | -0.47 | -1.11% | | | 1-17 16 00 |
| GIG | GIG | 1.63 | -0.03 | -1.81% | Technology | Semiconductors | 1-17 16 00 |
| HPTO | HPTO | 0.30 | -0.01 | -3.17% | Technology | Software | 1-17 16 00 |
| ITB | ITB | 24.09 | -0.33 | -1.35% | | | 1-17 16 00 |
| JOF | JOF - Japan | 9.10 | +0.07 | 0.78% | | | 1-17 16 00 |
| KOL | KOL trading portfolio | 18.38 | +0.04 | 0.22% | | | 1-17 16 00 |
| MTSI | M/A-Com Technology Solutions Holdings Inc. (MTSI) | 16.25 | +0.06 | 0.37% | Technology | Semiconductors | 1-17 16 00 |
| MSD | MSD | 9.57 | -0.03 | -0.31% | | | 1-17 16 00 |
| MTSI | MTSI | 16.25 | +0.06 | 0.37% | Technology | Semiconductors | 1-17 16 00 |
| NICE | NICE - Innovators | 42.04 | -0.39 | -0.92% | Technology | Telecom Equipment | 1-17 16 00 |
| PAMT | PAMT | 15.57 | -0.48 | -2.99% | Technology | Electronic Equipment | 1-17 16 00 |
| RYN | RYN - realestate | 41.91 | +0.53 | 1.28% | Financial | Specialty REITs | 1-17 16 00 |
| TROX | TROX | 23.33 | +0.04 | 0.17% | Materials | Specialty Chemicals | 1-17 16 00 |
| USCR | USCR | 21.97 | +0.01 | 0.05% | Industrial | Building Materials | 1-17 16 00 |

On the weekends and in mid-week I check out the charts listed here. I have, at one time or another, traded every company symbol listed above.

I have just purchased TROX and will list the chart along with my reasoning for the purchase.

The only question TROX asks is has it started a stage 2 or is it still in stage 1? The Power Pop is certainly full blown and the movement upward was speedy before it turned into a consolidation. That may be stalling out at the top of a stage 1. For this to be a money maker it has to truck it on into a strong stage 2. I am looking for something around $25.50 or higher. If it doesn't move all I can hope for is just a break even. It is not a gamble but a risk. Risks are a given when stocks are bought and sold. At times they work and at other times they don't. Make your risks win more then they lose.

The End

Visit my website http://www.manageyourowntrades.com/ to follow my current trades and for more information.

## Excerpt from my website for the Client's Categories, Tracking and Research

All Clients Real & Potential

SITE WILL BE UPDATED DAILY ON THE PORTFOLIO STOCKS. If you select the symbol you will see the stocks I own or have just sold. The updated text will be made current each week..

This site is primarily set up for small investors with portfolio investing capabilities from two hundred fifty to five thousand dollar amounts. The upper limit investors can follow my investing regimen but the two hundred fifty dollar accounts will keep each purchase under $100 and trade only when their accounts contain $100 or more. Remember, at Scottrade you will be charged seven dollars per trade and need to figure that amount into your purchase price. No, you won't make much money but if you get good and lucky maybe your account will grow too much larger proportions. Also, the percentages are the same. Thirty percent of a million dollar trade is the same increase as thirty percent of a one hundred dollar trade. Just not near as much cash in the pocket.

.

Remember I am explaining how I trade, no guarantees that they will work for you. The information in this article is for educational purposes only and should not be construed as a recommendation to buy or sell the stocks mentioned.

When looking at the trades, Red stands for ALERT about that stock. Green will be good news.

My trading philosophy. I remember from other market corrections both great and small that some stocks did well in those markets. No longer am I going to worry about a big market drop. Just keep up with my research and go short and long on individual stocks. Not because of what the market is doing, but what each stock appears to be doing. No more trying to predict the market. I will adhere to the Dow and DAQ theories in order to know whether the market is strong or week. I am going to add the stocks I have traded to the end of this section. I will show a running total of my trades there. I will also have the Dow Theory available for your edification.

Check out the Dow Theory read chart top to bottom.

AWRE- 12/31: It is time to dump. Total gain for year = $16.23 = 3% gain. 1/22: Just plugging along in a consolidation but all positive so if it breaks up it will be buy. Still not ready to trade,

CME: 12/30: Stopped out with a 15% gain. Everything went negative and heading for a negative Power Pop. Still negative.

CRDS: 12/30 Bought 100s @ $2.4283 - Total: $249.83. After a great Power Pop. On 1/23 = I am watching for that first red candle. Still green candle in a down NASDAQ. Let her go

EXTR – 12/31 -Stock subject in my book (available at Amazon.com- The Power Pop Investor). 01/23/14: The Kiss and Tell has Kissed and told. Now we are making a little money.

FARO: 1/15 Bought 20s @ $57.3399 – Total: $1160.  Stopped out 20s – Total: $1,109.98 . equal total loss of 50.82 for 5% loss.  1/23/14 I'm out. minus 5% but there will be another day for FARO. Re-learned a lesson here.  Wait until near closing to trade.

HXL: This is an issue Nova is recommended.  It is so positive I am a believer.  Bought 25s @ $46.2599 – Total: $1,163.50

IWSY – This has cost me almost $400 so far.  1/4/14 just today in a power pop buy.  Stock price got well above the DMA and flattened out so I am still out.

LODE: 1/23 My gold hedge finally back to breakeven but it doesn't matter because I'm holding this for the gold value.

## About the Author of The Power Pop Investor

Don L. Markham presents some of the interesting methods he uses for making charting images and systems real. He makes them tell an understandable story. Each stock has a pictorial representation about itself. The methods he introduces makes the old maxim, "a picture is worth a thousand words", seem absolutely true. A quick scan of the information and visuals contained in this book will encourage the reader to get in on the action on the market.

The Power Pop Investor
ISBN: 9781467598682

www.ingramcontent.com/pod-product-compliance
Lightning Source LLC
Chambersburg PA
CBHW040816200526
45159CB00024B/3002